Learning to Live With OCD and Anxiety
"separating myths from facts"

by Katie Mercer

I0102962

Dedication

This book is dedicated in memory to my Nan,
Iris Whitten

Learning to Live With OCD and Anxiety
"*separating myths from facts*"

by Katie Mercer

ISBN-13: 978-1987902402
ISBN-10: 1987902408

Published in Canada

Copyrights

Acknowledgments

Thank you to my editor, proofreaders, and cover artist for your support:

~ Katie ~

Katherine McCarthy of Aeternum Designs (book cover), Bettye McKee (editor), RJ Parker, Lorrie Suzanne Phillippe, Marlene Fabregas, Robyn MacEachern, Kathi Garcia, Vicky Matson-Carruth, Linda H. Bergeron, Sandra Miller, Valerie Hartling, Patricia Lenckus, Lee Knieper Husemann, Gail Chen, Laura Martin and Laura Swain

Table of Contents

Introduction

According to the health statistics generated by the BBC, one in every fifty American citizens is suffering from obsessive compulsive disorder (OCD). The ones suffering from this disorder sometimes feel isolated from their families and friends, but there actually is a good deal of support available in the community surrounding them. To ensure a better life quality, the most important thing is developing sufficient knowledge about this mental illness. This is necessary due to the fact that people suffering from this kind of disorder usually experience different kinds of obsessions as well as compulsions. These emotions are very strong and dominating, yet the sufferer does not have any control over them. So when the sufferer becomes aware of the fact that their entire condition is nothing but simply an illusion or a state of mind, they get better at dealing with it.

People suffering from this health problem go through obsessive worries or doubts that strongly interfere with their living. OCD is known to be a state of mental illness while it technically is a kind of brain disorder. The sufferers describe their condition as mental hiccups, as they believe their minds often get fixated on a certain event, like washing hands, so they keep thinking about and doing the same things.

Some of the people with OCD get cured completely after going through the right kind of treatment. On the other hand, some of them usually enjoy a significant relief from the intense condition while still having OCD in their system. The usual treatments normally are comprised of medications as well as lifestyle changes. This combination is known to be highly effective, as it works on the sufferer's body and mind at the same time.

What is OCD?

OCD stands for Obsessive Compulsive Disorder. It is a mental condition experienced by people belonging to different age groups and different walks of life. The person suffering from obsessive compulsive disorder gets caught in an endless loop of compulsions and obsessions. Obsessions may be referred to as intrusive, unwanted thoughts, urges or images. However, they trigger some strongly distressing feelings as well.

Compulsions, on the other hand, may be referred to as behaviors that some individuals engage in as a response to the obsession in order to eliminate or reduce their distress. Most people experience obsessive thoughts in association with compulsive behaviors during some time in their lives. But this doesn't mean that they all have OCD. When it's about diagnosing this illness, the above-mentioned cycle of both obsessions as well as compulsions get so extreme that it takes up a good amount of the sufferer's time and thus keeps them from performing important daily activities.

As discussed above, not every habit or ritual may be considered a compulsion. Almost every one of us sometimes like to double-check certain things. But what differentiates a normal person from one suffering from OCD are the following symptoms:

OCD sufferers cannot control their thoughts or behaviors even when they recognize that those thoughts or behaviors are excessive.

They spend at least one hour every day on such obsessive thoughts or behaviors. They don't experience any pleasure while performing the obsessive rituals. What they feel is just a relief from their anxiety.

They experience certain problems while living their daily life due to such obsessions and compulsions.

Some of the individuals having OCD also sometimes experience a tic disorder. There are motor tics and vocal tics. Motor tics are usually brief, sudden repetitive movements like shoulder or head jerking, shoulder shrugging, facial grimacing and different kinds of eye movements. On the other hand, vocal tics include repetitive grunting sounds, sniffing, throat clearing, etc.

Symptoms also change on a regular basis. They keep coming and going, getting better or worse over time. People suffering from OCD may help themselves by trying to avoid the situations that are known to trigger their obsessions. They may also use some kind of drugs or alcohol to calm themselves. Although a majority of us who do suffer from OCD usually recognize that we aren't making any sense by doing these irrational things, some of the adults and most of the children never realize that their behavior isn't ordinary or normal. Different kinds of symptoms are usually recognized in children by their parents or teachers.

In case someone believes they are going through the obsessive compulsive disorder, the best course of action is talking to an experienced doctor who understands different aspects of this condition. This is important because this disorder has the ability to interfere with every single aspect of the sufferer's life when left untreated.

Types of Obsessive-Compulsive Disorder

The Diagnostic and Statistical Manual (DSM) for mental disorders offers an extensive definition on the obsessive compulsive disorder. It includes the presence of both obsessions as well as compulsions that may cause a major disruption or distress to the patient's daily living. However, people experience different symptoms in totally different ways that largely differ from other sufferers. Researchers and clinicians suggest that the obsessive compulsive disorder may be divided into various types on the basis of how they are usually experienced by different people.

Contamination obsessions along with cleaning and washing compulsions

When a person is affected by such a disorder, they normally focus upon different feelings of discomfort that are related to contamination and excessive cleaning and washing. For instance, a sufferer may feel that their hands are contaminated or they will contaminate other people with their germs. In order to get rid of the worry, the sufferer usually needs to wash their hands repetitively for several hours. A list of different things that trigger the symptoms in a person suffering from obsessive compulsive disorder is given below.

> Using public washrooms
> Cleaning of bathroom and kitchen
> Excessive tooth brushing
> Clothes
> Avoiding red stains and objects
> Being surrounded by people
> Touching poles
> Touching a banister on a staircase
> Doing laundry in a laundromat
> Eating in a restaurant or a café
> Visiting hospitals
> Waiting in a GP's clinic
> Using public payphones
> Touching handles or door knobs
> Shaking hands
> Contact with chemicals

Harmful obsessions along with different checking compulsions

A person suffering from this kind of symptom usually experiences certain intensive thoughts about bringing harm to themselves or others. In order to cater to these feelings, the sufferer usually carries out different checking rituals in order to relieve their distress. For instance, the person might believe that their house is burning, so they may want to continually drive by their house in order to ensure that nothing bad is happening. Moreover, they may also feel that by giving a certain disastrous event some thought, the chances for such an event's likelihood may increase. Some things that might trigger the obsessive compulsive disorder in people suffering from these kinds/types of symptoms usually experience are listed below:

Electric or gas stove knobs
Water taps
Door locks
House alarm
Windows
Appliances
House lights
Car doors
Greeting cards and postal letters
Candles
Purse or wallet
People
Schizophrenia
Rereading certain lines or words in a book
Memory
Driving routes
Symptoms and illnesses
Reassurance

Uncontrolled obsessions

This kind of symptom usually relates to different unwanted obsessions related to aggressive, religious or sexual themes. For instance, one might experience intrusive thoughts regarding being an attacker or even a rapist. The person may use a number of different mental rituals, like praying, recitation, counting, etc. in order to relieve their anxiety while going through involuntary thoughts. Triggers associated with such kinds of obsessions are normally avoided regardless of the price that needs to be paid for that.

Obsessions along with compulsions related to counting, arranging and ordering

A person who experiences different symptoms usually develops a strong urge for arranging and rearranging different objects until they believe these to be perfectly well oriented. For instance, a person may feel the requirement for constantly arranging their shirts in such a way that they are in precise order according to their colors. Such kinds of symptoms may also include thinking or even actually saying different words or sentences repeatedly until they accomplish the task in the perfect way.

Sometimes, counting, arranging and ordering compulsions are usually carried out in order to ward off the potential danger. For instance, one may believe that their family will die in some kind of accident unless they arrange their desk or cupboard in the perfect way.

Hoarding

According to the DSM 5, hoarding is now recognized as a unique and distinct diagnosis. Hoarding incorporates a whole collection of different items that are believed to have limited value by others. People suffering from such symptoms usually get obsessed with different low-valued items like old magazines, containers, notes, junk mail, receipts, clothes, etc. The living space of people with such symptoms usually gets so cluttered and messy that it becomes almost impossible to live in.

Hoarding is sometimes accompanied by different obsessional fears, like losing different possessions or items that you may require one day. Moreover, it also causes people to develop an emotional attachment to different objects.

Those who are affected by hoarding usually experience a higher level of depression and anxiety in comparison to people suffering from OCD. They are also sometimes incapable of holding a steady job. More importantly, it is also possible for compulsive hoarding to occur without having the obsessive compulsive disorder.

Overlapping Symptoms and Types of OCD

Although different symptoms turn out to become more stable with the passage of time, there is also a possibility for a change in the focus and nature of the symptoms. Moreover, there is also a good chance for a person to keep experiencing certain symptoms on a regular basis while developing other similar symptoms at the same time.

In a general perspective, a majority of the symptoms of obsessive compulsive disorder respond well to different combinations of medications, exposure response prevention, and cognitive behavior therapy. One of the exceptions in this regard is hoarding, as it is not known to have any improvements with medication, but it responds reasonably enough to different psychotherapies. If a person is suffering from any symptom associated with obsessive compulsive disorder, the best and the most appropriate course of action is to consult an experienced medical practitioner, like a physician or a psychologist, and taking a combination of treatments, such as Cognitive Behavior Treatment (CBT) and Exposure and Response Prevention (ERP), which may be adjusted by the doctor to suit the needs of the sufferer according to the symptoms they have.

Typical Obsessions

Obsessions may be referred to as unwanted, intrusive and recurrent images, impulses or thoughts that may cause anxiety to a person. At first, the person may experience obsessions as relatively benign, while over the passage of time, they may be associated with uncontrolled anxiety and fear. Following are the most common obsessions experienced by people:

Contamination
Bodily fluids like feces, urine
Disease and germs like HIV, herpes
Environmental contaminants, like asbestos, radiation
Household chemicals, like solvents and cleaners
Dirt

Unwanted sexual thoughts
Perverse or forbidden images or sexual thoughts
Perverse or forbidden sexual impulses about other people
Obsessions related to homosexuality
Incest or sexual obsessions involving minors
Obsessions towards aggressive sexual behavior

Losing control

Fear of acting upon an impulse for harming oneself

Fear of acting upon an impulse for harming others

Fear of horrific or violent images in a person's mind

Fear of blurting out insults or obscenities

Fear of stealing items

Harm

Fear of being responsible for a terrible happening

Fear of harming other people

Perfectionism related obsessions

Concerns about exactness or evenness

Concerns about remembering or needing to know something

Fear of forgetting or losing important information

Inability to decide whether to discard or keep different things

Fear of losing of different things

Religious obsessions
Concerns about blasphemy
Concerns about offending the Almighty God
Concerns about morality
Concerns about what's right or wrong

Other obsessions
Concerns about getting a disease or a physical illness
Having superstitious ideas

Different people have different symptoms of obsessive compulsive disorder. It is not important for a person suffering from it to have indications similar to another person who is also suffering from it. People normally experience only one or two symptoms, but sometimes they may have more. OCD is very alarming and it needs to be taken care of immediately; otherwise, it may prevent the sufferer from performing their routine duties in the correct way. A combination of medication in corporation with different kinds of therapies may turn out to be a very viable and effective solution in this regard.

Typical Compulsions

Obsessive Compulsive Disorder is one of the major health issues these days. It is a mental disorder that can affect any one of us, at any age, and in any part of the world. It occurs when you are caught up in the loop of compulsions and obsessions. These obsessions are the unwanted thoughts, urges or images that can accelerate the upsetting feelings. On the other hand, compulsions are what a person does to get rid of the obsession, or, to be precise, get rid of the stress he is suffering from.

Two percent of Americans are suffering from obsessive compulsive disorder. Many of them feel like they are alone and their friends aren't with them or their families aren't happy about them. Well, proper knowledge on OCD is vital for those who are living their lives with this condition and the ones who are helping them or providing help when needed. If you already know what it is, you are way ahead in understanding how to deal with people suffering from such mental illness. Also, it is the fastest way to improve the patient's quality of living.

One who is always in doubt and worried about something that interferes with his life completely may be suffering from it. In technical terms, it is a brain disorder, but it is still considered as a mental illness. A common symptom is the need to do something that has no value to others, such as washing hands repeatedly to get rid of bacteria. Some people can be completely cured after the treatment. On the other hand, some may still have this condition but in a less acute form compared to what it was before. But treatment isn't one dimensional since it covers both medication as well as a changed lifestyle.

People suffering from this illness may be afraid of dirt, germs, toxins and other similar things and thus clean themselves relentlessly. They may also think of harming others and even themselves. At the same time, they may have excessive sexual urges as well as thoughts. Some people may think that they should confess each and everything they think or do. They are very much conscious about placing things, and they take good care that all the things are arranged in their particular places.

The common signs of OCD are repeatedly checking whether the door is opened or closed and washing hands again and again. Apart from that, there are many other forms in which these compulsions may take place, such as counting items, checking lights, praying, repeating something many times, arranging things as they were and hoarding. There is no problem in doing all these things. But what makes the situation worse is repeating the process again and again. People with OCD just can't stop themselves from doing these things over and over again.

Obsessions and Compulsions

People with Obsessive Compulsive Disorder are obsessed with unwanted impulses, thoughts or images which can result in tremendous anxiety and are often disturbing. Living with OCD and anxiety can have significant impact on one's mental and physical health. It is a debilitating illness but is treatable. Read further to get a closer look at compulsions and obsessions.

Both compulsions and obsessions involve a disaster. This gives few people an impression that they are more or less alike. Obsession is a mental disorder which refers to repetitive impulses or ideas in the mind of an individual. These impulses and ideas make the person mentally unbalanced by being persistent. Although the person with obsession does not really want to obsess about something, she or he still has ideas that keeps popping into their head pretty often. Although the person is occupied with other things, the idea would recur and disrupt their entire thought process.

A compulsion is also one type of mental disorder. Nevertheless, it involves an action of some kind. Obsession just involves ideas and impulses. However, a compulsion is a bit different. The person suffering from a compulsion disorder repeats a particular action often that she or he is fixated on. This repetitive action tends to become a daily ritual for such a person. The person dealing with this disorder does not cease to have the urge to indulge into a particular action, and hence it ends up being a ritual.

An obsession can actually result in a compulsion on the contrary. Any person who is fixated by an action would certainly be having an obsession. For instance, a person who has a compulsion of washing hands often may be obsessed with maintaining high levels of hygiene. This explains the reason for a particular compulsion. In such instance, it would not be wrong to say that the person is clearly manifesting an obsession through a compulsion. Obsession is limited to the mind whereas compulsion is characterized by an action. A compulsion involves persistent actions whereas an obsession involves persistent ideas.

Obsessions and compulsions are the two main symptoms of Obsessive Compulsive Disorder. These can hinder one's daily life as well as reduce the overall quality of life. An obsession is normally seen as irrational and is intrusive. However, the person suffering from this disorder cannot ignore or stop these thoughts. Some common obsessions include consistently worrying whether the stove was turned off before leaving the house or worrying about becoming sick from germs. People who have OCD feel fear in addition to obsessive thoughts. Sometimes, obsessions remain in the back of the mind and occur once in a while. However, some times the obsessive thoughts turn out to be constant. These thoughts can intrude into the quality of one's life. These have been known to bring a strain on relationships as well as at the workplace. The fear of becoming ill, fear of dirt, having constant thoughts of a certain number and the need to have something done in a certain way or certain order are some of the examples of obsessions that people face generally.

Obsessions are more of recurrent actions, compulsions and thoughts. In most of the cases, these seem mild, but in some cases, these turn out to be extreme. These develop when people are trying to relieve themselves from obsessive thoughts. For instance, a person may continually wash their hands where there is an obsession with germs. They would continue doing that to the point their hands become raw from washing. Obsessions may go away for a short period, but normally these tend to come back. Compulsions begin again once obsessions return, thereby kicking into a cycle of obsession and compulsion.

Compulsions can significantly interfere with the life of a person. For instance, one may end up losing sleep when they feel the urge to check whether or not the doors are locked over and over again. Brushing teeth, washing hands, checking to see if the doors are locked, checking to see if the appliances have been turned off, requiring constant approval from people around are some of the common examples of compulsions.

This anxiety disorder can be treated with behavioral therapy and also with medications. However, obsessions and compulsions share an interrelationship. Obsessions lead to compulsions, or it can be stated that compulsions occur as a result of obsessions. Obsessions tend to cause worry, deep anxiety and fear. Compulsions may result in bodily damage. However, both tend to cause disruptions in the day-to-day life of the person impacted.

Obsessions result in thoughts that are inappropriate, senseless and often irrational which cannot be controlled by the person. This can trigger serious anxiety in him or her. A compulsion is more of a behavior exhibited by a person that may help them deal with the anxiety caused by obsessions. The tabular comparison below clarifies the exact differences between obsessions and compulsions. These will help you gain a better insight into where lies the difference while defining compulsions and obsessions.

	Compulsion
Definition	The state or action of being forced or forcing oneself to do something An irresistible urge to behave in a particular manner
Description	Feeling compelled to do something over and over again
In psychology	Behaviors help people in dealing with anxiety
Interrelationship	Are a result of obsessions
Effects	Can result in bodily harm or any kind of inconvenience
Examples	Washing hands every now and then, shaking leg, knocking on a door three times before entering, fixing things that seem out of place

Relation Between Obsessions and Compulsions

Schizophrenia is known as a psychotic mental disorder that manifests through difficulties in thinking, behavior and mood. It can be based on positive or negative symptoms. Positive symptoms are characterized by hallucinations and delusions, and negative symptoms through alogia, affective flattening, anhedonia, avolition and asociality. OCS (obsessive compulsive symptoms) present in schizophrenia is known as a part of the definition of this mental illness. Having OCS in the prodromal time of schizophrenia protects the person affected with the psychotic symptoms of the illness and helps slow the progress of schizophrenia. Other studies have also shown that having these symptoms can play a role in protecting against psychotic symptoms. It is known that this occurs in 30% to 59% of all enduring with schizophrenia.

Schizophrenia along with OCS creates another disorder which is known as schizo-obsessive disorder. Since all these symptoms, like delusions, obsessions, compulsions and stereotypes, occur at once, studying this disorder seems very difficult. It has been observed that OCS occur after treatment with atypical antipsychotic. However, there is not enough evidence of how this affects schizophrenia.

The relation of OCS and positive and negative symptoms of schizophrenia showed results that contradict themselves. In some results, those with OCS present more positive symptoms than those who don't have it. Another result presented high positive similarities of delusions and obsessions, and that of auditory hallucinations and compulsions. In correlation to these results, it seems that those who suffer from auditory hallucinations and people with OCD interpret thoughts the same way.

In other studies, the results showed that negative symptoms on schizophrenia with OCS are less in those without these symptoms. One study conducted on the first stage of schizophrenia showed that there are lower levels of flat affect sub-scale for negative symptoms in the schizo-obsessive group when compared to those of the other group. However, the result was contrary in another case; the negative symptoms in people with schizophrenia and OCS were more. These results showed that the co-occurrence of schizophrenia and OCD needed a special clinical picture. But without enough clear results, the state of this finding remained unknown. In a study where the results of several studies were compared on those with schizophrenia and OCS without OCD, more serious psychotic symptoms were observed compared to schizophrenia without OCS, where there were differences in OCD schizophrenia and non-OCD schizophrenia. It states that if a classic definition was presented instead of OCS without the use of OCD, there would be less OCS in the control group, and this could result in less effects of compulsion and obsession on the level of psychotic symptoms.

The reason for these contradictions could be the differences among the methods used and the amount of time those who were suffering from the illness; thus, more research needs to be done on OCS in schizophrenic patients to analyze the results of the symptoms, psychotic symptoms, and social and cognitive characteristics.

Signs & Symptoms

Are you the type of person who likes everything to be clean and arranged in a specific order or can't sleep if all the doors and windows are not locked? These behaviors are usually considered normal or just the way the personality of a person works. However, sometimes it can mean that you have obsessive-compulsive disorder. It is a condition described as compulsions and obsessive thoughts that affect many people. Here are a few signs that might help you figure out if you really have OCD.

Hand washing or using hand sanitizer compulsively is known to be a big characteristic of people with OCD. It is a fear of microbes, which is the most observed cause of obsession. It can also be viewed as the fear of making others sick or feeling filthy.

Is your house clean all the time? Cleanliness is good, but too much of it is definitely not. Some people with tend to keep everything spotless. This is similar to those who wash their hands continuously, fearing microbes and the feel of impurity. Cleaning can cease the symptoms of OCD, but it's highly likely that next time, the urge will be even stronger.

The urge to check things, coming back four, five, or even more times to make sure the door is locked, ensuring the alarm is set several times, etc. are some behaviors very common in people with OCD. The reason for these behaviors comes from several things, like the fear of being hurt or the lack of responsibility.

Some behaviors of people with OCD are associated with specific numbers or even counting through daily tasks. The reason behind this is caused by superstitions; for example, the feeling that a specific number protects them or someone else, or if they don't turn the light on and off three times, something bad will happen to them.

Another aspect of people with OCD is that they feel everything needs to be perfectly organized, symmetric and in order.

Thoughts of inappropriate or sexual acts often happen in OCD. People have thoughts of molesting a minor or inappropriately touching someone or even being concerned about their sexual orientation.

Another interesting behavior is that people with OCD analyze their relationships and experiences with friends or any other person they personally know. They can spend hours on the same thought about how a specific moment made them or someone else feel bad.

People with OCD tend to calm themselves by asking others about their thoughts on something. If they feel bad about something that happened yesterday, they will continue to ask a friend about it to get assurance that it was fine.

Body dysmorphic disorder or BDD is a condition that people with OCD can have and thus they may believe that a part of their bodies is not attractive. BDD is very similar to OCD in the way the obsessive thoughts occur.

Symptoms of OCD differ from person to person, but there is a specific pattern of behaviors and thoughts.

This pattern is made of four steps:

Obsession of a thought that is stressing and keeps going through your mind.

Anxiety happens exactly when obsession begins.

Compulsion is the mental or physical behavior that keeps repeating itself and is caused by anxiety as a way of relief.

Temporary relief is when the compulsive behavior helps you get rid of the anxicty, but the obsessive thoughts will come back and the anxiety will be often stronger.

Obsessive Thoughts

Everyone experiences unpleasant thoughts during their lifetime and some more than others, like the fear that the gas oven is turned on and thus the house will burn down.

However, when you have repetitive and persistent thoughts that won't get out of your mind, it is highly possible that you are obsessive.

Obsessive thoughts are characterized as the fear of something or that everything needs to be perfect. Here are a few examples of obsessions common in people with OCD:

The fear of hurting yourself or someone else by accident, like when you fear that the cat will go out and get hurt because the door is left open.

The fear of intentionally hurting yourself or someone else, like when you hit someone.

The fear of getting microbes of being contaminated with a disease.

A requirement that everything needs to be in order, like arranging skittles by color before eating them.

Compulsive Behavior

Compulsions are the acts that someone with OCD does to avoid anxiety caused by an obsession. However, this behavior usually has nothing to do with the actual reason of the behavior.

For example, someone may have the fear that if they step on the sidewalk lines, something bad will happen to a loved one. Or if they step on a line by mistake, they would think that a person whom they like would get hurt soon.

People with OCD are aware that these behaviors are absurd and make no sense; however, they cannot get rid of these and feel like they have to do these, worrying about what if these are true and something bad will really happen.

Most people affected by OCD will gain other mental problems and some may be more serious than others, such as:

Behaviors that affect the way you eat can cause eating disorders, thus leading to weight gain or loss and other health issues.

Most people who have OCD have or had episodes of depression. It is very common that depression is accompanied by OCD and they come hand in hand most of the time.

Getting attached to objects, even the most useless ones, and avoiding throwing them away. Even if you never use these objects and they have no role at all, you feel that they have to be kept in a box somewhere.

General anxiety by various reasons and even the smallest mistake or event can lead to hours of anxiety.

Causes and Anxiety

Many people are eager to know about the actual causes of OCD. Well, it may amaze you that the real reasons have not yet been identified. A lot of research has been going on for years, but still scientists have not been able to point out the exact causes.

However, many scientists believe that OCD is the result of a combination of different factors including genetic, cognitive, neurobiological, behavioral and environmental factors which may cause this disorder at any point of time. Mentioned below are some of the main causes of OCD as estimated by modern science.

Biological Factors

In many cases, biological factors play a major role of causing this disorder. It has been seen that specific parts of the brains of OCD sufferers are different as compared to those of non-sufferers, yet, it isn't still known how these obvious differences are related to OCD. When it's about biological factors, the focus is kept on the circuit that actually regulates the basic aspects of our thoughts, such as sexuality, aggression, excretions, etc. The circuit transfers information from the front part of the brain named as orbitofrontal cortex to the other part of the brain named as thalamus. As soon as the circuit is activated, you get attentive towards certain things and thus you cannot control yourself but to perform those particular actions.

For example, in our everyday lives, we go to the washroom and before going out, we wash our hands. When you think you are done, the signal is passed to the brain and you stop washing your hands and go out of the washroom. But if you are suffering from OCD, it will be difficult for your brain to turn off that circuit, and thus it will be in your mind all the time. As a result, you will be washing your hands for a longer period of time and you may also repeat the process again and again.

Psychological Factors

Behavioral and cognitive theories are supported by many psychiatrists to identify the real reasons of psychological factors.

The behavioral theory states that people with OCD have fear in their mind and hence they perform things to avoid it. The question is, when does this fear begin? One probability is a time of huge stress. It can be during the starting of a whole new life or may be the ending of a relationship. In these situations, the chances of developing anxiety and fear are huge.

Things regarded as neutral in normal times may give birth to the feeling of fear during stressful times. For example, although a person may have been using public toilets for a long time, he may feel like he will get germs or illness under stress if he uses one. Now, when this connection of fear is established, he might tend to avoid using public toilets, no matter how much it is necessary for him. If he still uses it for urgency, he will perform different unusual acts, such as cleaning the toilet seat for a longer period of time. By doing certain actions, the fear will be removed for some time, but it will never be removed completely.

On the other hand, cognitive theory discusses about how people associate fear and object. This theory focuses primarily on the thoughts of people with OCD. It is highly possible that normal people can also have such thoughts, and many of them are able to get rid of these thoughts. However, people with OCD start taking these thoughts seriously. As a result, anxiety and certain emotions are common among them, such as disgust, guilt and shame. At this point, they try to neutralize their thoughts or avoid the thoughts, though they cannot.

This theory states that as long as people are attached to such thoughts, they will be stressed out. Some start having such thoughts because of false beliefs or negative incidents that happened in their lives. Some of the beliefs that play a big part in the development of obsessions in one's mind are given below:

The belief that you are responsible for causing harm to others.

The belief that certain thoughts with no real value are important and should be controlled.

The belief that thinking too much will make it come true.

The belief that you are perfect and mistakes are not welcomed.

Stress

Stress itself is not the major explanation for this illness, but the stressful event has a role to play. For example, if you were involved in or witnessed a road accident, chances are that OCD will develop in you. Moreover, it will get worse if not treated on time.

Genetic

Some recent studies have shown that many of the OCD sufferers have developed this condition due to genetic reasons. However, this theory has not yet been established as a fact, but it is assumed that genetics play an important role similar to what stress and psychological factors do.

Depression

Depression is another factor that can cause OCD in many cases. Many medical professionals believe that it is a symptom rather than a cause. Psychoanalytic theory suggests that there must have been some unconscious conflicts and discomforts in the early period of the patient's life that eventually gave rise to OCD.

However, no one knows what the actual causes are or what the factors are that result in it. There are many theories, but none can prove it with absolute certainty. It is highly possible that even ordinary life events or illnesses may induce the symptoms.

Related Disorders

There are some mental health issues associated with OCD because the condition involves repetitive urges, behaviors or thoughts. There are several habit disorders associated with it. Researchers have long believed that several conditions that can be seen in an individual suffering from OCD are linked to the disorders which are referred to as the OCD-spectrum of disorders. These include Compulsive skin picking, Body Dysmorphic Disorder, Trichotillomania and Tourette syndrome.

It is believed that the Body Dysmorphic Disorder is the closest of all OCD-spectrum disorders to the condition. Other conditions can be categorized as different conditions in their own right. The common factor in all the conditions in the OCD spectrum is that they involve the presence of repetitive urges, behaviors or thoughts to some degree. Many individuals with these conditions display OCD-type symptoms and are also co-morbid. This is the reason why these conditions are referred to as related disorders. When two such diagnoses are noted within a same individual, they are referred to as co-morbid.

Most of the disorders in the OCD-spectrum are hard to recognize, and this is the reason why these remain undiagnosed. The reason is that the symptoms mimic several other disorders such as panic disorder, agoraphobia, social phobia and other secondary conditions that fall in the Generalized Anxiety Disorder range. These can result in depression.

There are several other disorders that impact people suffering from OCD, even though they are not present in the OCD-spectrum disorders. These parallel the condition and are often considered to be a consequence. These include self-harm, panic attacks, emetophobia and depression. The subsequent paragraph offers an insight into the OCD-related disorders. Basic information about the related conditions has been offered that is generally noted in individuals.

Body Dysmorphic Disorder [BDD]

This is an anxiety disorder which is related to the body image of an individual. This is an image disorder characterized by intrusive and persistent preoccupations with slight or imagined defect in the appearance of an individual. People with this condition find fault with their stomach, nose, skin, hair or any other body part. This results in difficulties in daily functioning and severe emotional distress.

Compulsive Skin Picking

This is related to repetitive picking of the skin for relieving urges or anxiety. It can be experienced generally as a part of body Dysmorphic disorder.

Trichotillomania

This is a compulsive urge experienced by an individual which involves pulling the hair.

Obsessive Compulsive Personality Disorder [OCPD]

This condition is sometimes confused with OCD. However, it is not the same. This condition is more of a personality disorder.

Co-morbidity or being diagnosed by two or more conditions at the same time is quite commonly noted with OCD. This can make it difficult to diagnose and treat it. For instance, a person with OCD may be experiencing other mental health issues such as depression or anxiety. Only a thorough diagnosis can reveal the exact conditions impacting an individual suffering from it.

Myths and Facts

Obsessive Compulsive Disorder is a mental anxiety disorder recognized by psychiatrists from all around the world. It is defined by symptoms that include unwanted, beyond control recurrence of certain thoughts and/or compulsive and repetitive behaviors.

Expression of Obsessions and Compulsions: About 80% of the people suffering from OCD are troubled by both compulsions and obsessions. The remaining 20% suffer from either compulsion(s) or obsession(s).

In the case of people with exclusively compulsive or exclusively obsessive traits, there might exist a kind of hidden or restricted expression of the other trait. For example, if a person has only obsessions and no compulsions, there is a possibility that the compulsion-like responses (not defined compulsions) to those obsessions may occur, and vice versa. In response to obsessive urges, a person might use certain behaviours which are not obvious and discernible, such as suppressing the thoughts, avoiding the urge, behavioral maneuvering, and mental neutralizing strategies, etc.

Similarly, a person with exclusive compulsions might have suppressed obsession-like thoughts that are difficult to describe, such as constant feelings of 'something being wrong.'

Common Obsessional Tendencies

There are various kinds of fears and concerns in the mind of a person with OCD, such as:

Fear of hurting someone.
Fear of committing solecism.
Fear of contamination.
Concern for behaving in an unsocial or unconventional manner.
Concern for symmetrical or exact arrangements.
A habit of getting overly circumspect.

Common Compulsions

People with OCD are troubled by certain uncontrollable compulsive urges like:

Desire for cleaning or washing.
Urge to arrange and organize everything in proper or certain order.
Checking repeatedly for any anomalies or aberrations.
Secretly hoarding or acquiring objects that are deemed useless and are of no value.
Tapping or touching.

Counting or repeating again and again.

About four million people in the USA alone live with this disorder. It is present in all age groups, from children to elderly, and common in all socioeconomic divisions. It generally begins at an age of 10 to 12 years or at teenage and early adulthood.

It might begin as a mild disorder which can appear and disappear repeatedly, but if ignored or left untreated, it might aggravate to severe levels, sometimes putting those and their near ones in dire jeopardy.

According to the World Health Organization (WHO), it is more common and prevalent in developed nations as compared to developing ones.

In the USA, about 1 adult in every 50 and 1 child in every 100 suffers from OCD.

Most facing this illness don't seek help or therapy for many years.

The average age of diagnosis of people with OCD is 19 years old.

People suffering from it are not "insane"; they may get such thoughts, though, because of their awareness of the fact that their behavior is irrational.

Anxiety and depression are two very common traits of people with OCD. They often feel there is exclusive irrationality and obsession in their thoughts and behavior which are peculiar only to them, so they feel hesitation in sharing their issues, often allowing the disorder to stay undiagnosed until the symptoms are clearly evident to others.

Facts on the Causes of OCD

No specific causes with absolute certainty have yet been determined, but several factors and developments are held accountable for it.

Psychosocial Causes: Many researchers have inferred that families or societies and cultures with stringent disciplinary practices might invoke OCD in its members. Another factor is a sense of responsibilities that one tends to feel at certain stages in life, especially when one has to undergo drastic and major changes in one's behavior and character. This may also bring about the introduction of OCD; e.g., when an adolescent reaches puberty, when a couple gets married or has a child or any such activities that can be referred to as life-changing experiences.

Biological Factor: Researchers claim with most certainty that OCD has a biological connection. The brain activity and composition of an OCD patient varies from that of a normal person.

Recent studies using PET (Positron Emitting Tomography) scans have confirmed that the brain activity patterns of a person with OCD is considerably different from a normal person or a person with any other kind of mental health issues In OCD, certain parts of a patient's brain show hyperactivity.

MRI (Magnetic Resonance Imaging) has shown less white matter in an OCD patient's brain as compared to other normal persons. The most common biochemical factor responsible for the disorder is the anomaly in metabolism of a neurotransmitter (chemicals that carry nerve impulses from one nerve to other) called serotonin. Apart from serotonin, glutamine and dopamine are other neurotransmitters associated with it.

Hereditary: OCD is also known to have hereditary traits; i.e., it can pass to a patient's descendants through his genetic lineage.

OCD can be Triggered

In many cases the OCD exists as a genetic predisposition but remains dormant until the disorder is triggered by some significant event in life. An infection may trigger its onset or some stressful event that brings a lot of anxiety and responsibility into one's life, e.g., having a baby, getting married, etc.

Facts about Treatment

OCD is a treatable disorder; effective medication and behavioral therapy techniques are available:

Three out of four people benefit from the behavioral therapy whereas medication only resolves the trouble for 6 out of 10 people with up to only 50% of reduction in the disorder symptoms.

Once the medication is stopped, about half of the people are likely to go back to the abandoned rituals and start showing symptoms again.

One out of every four people finds behavioral therapy too difficult to cope with.

OCD may occur in men and women equally.

Myths

Everybody Obsessed with Cleanliness has OCD

A person overly concerned with neatness and thus washing and cleaning repeatedly is a significant symptom associated with OCD, but sometimes being concerned with cleanliness, cleaning and washing repeatedly can be just a personality trait which may be easily confused with OCD.

A person with overly love or concern for cleanliness or neatness can choose not to do so just by controlling his habit. A person with OCD can't help it as his brain doesn't let him rest his fears, thereby constantly urging him to clean and wash.

People with OCD Consider Their Behavior Normal and Rational

It is a common thought that OCD sufferer's don't know what they are doing, that they believe in the righteousness of their tendencies, but in fact, most of the people suffering from ODC know very much about the irrationality and unconventionality of their actions; that is why they strive to behave normally in public, but their compulsions and obsessions just keep coercing them.

A Harmless Disorder

Many believe that OCD is a funny situation, especially the way media portrays it, but the truth is completely otherwise. OCD is a serious disorder, and having no control over one's eccentricity takes a great toll on one's psyche, sometimes resulting into depression and even suicidal thoughts. If left untreated, it may lead to a person's social alienation and may pose other dire consequences.

It's Just an Urge to Maintain Neat and Clean Order and is an Unnecessary Germ Phobia

The disorder is far more complicated than once thought. Apart from the obsession with cleanliness, there are a lot of other forms and symptoms associated with OCD, like acquiring and/or hoarding useless articles; going through constant fear of harming someone; fear of some mishap or behaving irrationally in public. These concerns can severely hinder the personality of any human being.

Stress is a Significant Cause

Many believe that stress might result into OCD. Although stress can exacerbate the situation or might even trigger it, stress is never the sole cause of it. In some cases where it is dormant or genetically predisposed but inactive, stress may trigger it, but OCD is not caused only by stress.

OCD is More Likely to Target Women

This is the vaguest myth that exists regarding OCD; men, women, children, young and old, from all races and ethnicities are equally susceptible to OCD, and it is found in all groups at almost the same rate.

Tests and Scans

Unlike most other diseases, it can't be diagnosed by blood tests or scans. It is a mental health issue judged by psychiatric analysis.

Lack of Will Power?

OCD patients' obsession is neither a personality trait or a developed habit; it is a disease that needs treatment. To abstain from such actions that most of them know are unconventional and irrational, will power is just not enough.

Relaxing or withdrawing from actions can't help them; they simply need treatment.

OCD is Not Treatable

A person with OCD can reach out for help and treatment that can lead him to a normal lifestyle. The treatment is available in the forms of therapy and medication.

Obsessive Compulsive Disorder Runs in Families

Obsessive Compulsive Disorder can prove to be a horrifying medical condition creating unrest in the entire family. It can be challenging and exhausting for loved ones and those who are frequently in the company of the sufferer. Obsessive compulsive disorder is a type of chronic illness and can be treated, hence it is possible to overcome it. The importance of including family and friends in this concern cannot be overestimated because the one suffering from it needs a lot of support to fight this condition.

One of the most important things to point out here is the lack of awareness that there are many people who know and care about someone suffering from OCD and are willing to help; however, due to the lack of information, they don't know what to do. It can be difficult for them to understand the situation; therefore, relationships may then be at risk. A family member affected by OCD affects the entire family. Sometimes it may be difficult for them to stay calm; thus negative environments may be created. In addition to it, financial and emotional burdens arise, adding to the problem already existing.

It may also affect the children, making it difficult for them to understand and cope with a person with OCD in the family. They may feel insecure as they would think that the patient is getting mad. The person affected by OCD needs regular support so that the illness can be treated and they can be normal again.

There are various combinations of family and friends affected by OCD that can be simplified as follows:

The partner of the OCD patient,
The parent of an adult patient with OCD,
The parent of a minor child with OCD,
The parent of a teenager with OCD,
The minor child of a parent suffering from OCD, or
The friends of the patient.

If someone is concerned with the well-being of the patient, he/she needs to gather as much information as possible regarding symptoms, treatment and other aspects of OCD. People should not feel they have to face this problem alone and must have the fullest support of their loved ones. There are many faces of this medical issue, and one needs to be well equipped with the right information to tackle it in every step.

It has been proven that the earlier one receives treatment, the higher the chances of success of the treatment. If you think that someone in your family or in your circle is showing the symptoms of OCD, you should motivate them to seek a doctor's help without any delays. If it's a child, you should take him/her to a general practitioner (GP). If the patient is a teenager, you should allow him or her to speak with your doctor alone. Although many people are already aware of OCD, there are still a number of doctors and OCD patients who don't know much about this illness. You as a friend, family or colleague should know the various stages of OCD treatment with Cognitive Behavioral Therapy (CBT).

For young people and children, the feelings of being the only one suffering and being alone can be challenging, thus causing the condition to seem even worse than it actually is. Clarification should be given to those who are suffering that they are not alone; there are many others suffering as well. Once a visit to the GP is made, he or she can then arrange an appointment with or transfer you to the local Child and Adolescent Mental Health Services (CAMHS). At this stage, you will be consulting a professional who will check the symptoms and try to diagnose the problem to start the treatment procedure. There are cases where people don't want to admit that they themselves are the unfortunate ones with OCD and that they are suffering from a mental disorder. Such circumstances result in a difficult state for the patient's loved ones who are trying to help him, thus resulting in distress.

To overcome this issue, the patient needs to know more about OCD by other means, such as by reaching out to others affected by this problem who are receiving treatment, journals and magazines regarding this issue, and any way to make the person feel that they should not feel embarrassed; this problem can be solved. The patient's family and friends can offer a helping hand so that he or she acknowledges the problem and starts receiving treatment as soon as possible.

While visiting healthcare professionals, the caretakers might be asked some questions regarding OCD. Also, they would be asked about their approaches to solving the problem. This is necessary because if the loved ones collude with them, it can act as a main reinforcement in treatment of this illness. They need to provide things like clean clothes, towels and meals as per their requirements.

OCD is not caused due to someone's fault since it is a mental disorder, and thus it should be dealt with accordingly. It should be solved together as a team with practical motivation. For example, it may be said by children that a school bully or a bad teacher is trying to make them do things that they don't like and their parents are going to take care of it as they do in real life. This would make them more confident, and this may also be the case in teenagers and adults. There should be a level of understanding regarding this issue between the patients and the ones taking care of them in order to discuss various symptoms that otherwise may cause the patient discomfort to discuss that could include thoughts of being connected to a crime, sexual thoughts or violence. It takes a high level of patience to tackle and remain focused on the procedure of recovery.

Obsessive Compulsive Disorder in Children

OCD is a common psychiatric illness that even impacts adolescents and children. This condition earlier impacted just one to three percent of people. However, it is now considered to be a common mental condition after substance abuse, depression and phobias. OCD peaks at two different phases of one's life: pre-adolescent and early stages of adulthood. The first peak of OCD cases is noted around the age of 10. This is the phase that overlaps with increasing presentation and school pressures. This phase is as well characterized with changes in body as well as brain. The second peak is noted in early adulthood, which is also considered to be the stage of developmental evolution when occupational and educational stresses tend to be high. Researchers have long argued that the OCD impacted during childhood represents a unique sub-type of disorder that has distinct characteristics.

Adults impacted with OCD would have experienced the onset of the condition during their childhood. Many of these would not even have realized that they have fallen prey to a mental condition. Several measures are being taken these days for increasing the recognition and awareness of this treatable condition in general population as well as in schools.

Symptoms of OCD are similar in adults and children. Individuals with it have repetitive images or thoughts. The anxiety caused by these repetitive thoughts result in actions or impulses that seem to be time-consuming or distressing. Obsessive thoughts can scare or upset kids, however. Teens and kids can feel powerless to stop focusing on these repetitive thoughts even if they wish to. This can make their life quite stressful. Fortunately, teens and kids can get better with the right care and attention.

OCD can be recognized through compulsive rituals and obsessions. Obsessive thoughts can compel kids and teens to act and feel irritable, sad, anxious or upset. Kids with the condition can get obsessed with:

Harm or illness from relatives.
Body wastes.
Having aggressive thoughts.
Whether objects contain germs or dirt.
Things being uneven or symmetrical.
Things being done in a specific manner.
Colors, sounds, words or numbers.

Kids with OCD tend to become afraid of what may happen if something is uneven or dirty. They tend to worry about things that may come true. They tend to believe that having bad thoughts may bring them bad luck. Obsessions make it quite difficult for them to enjoy activities or focus on schoolwork. Kids with OCD force themselves to be a part of specific rituals for getting respite from obsessive thoughts. These may involve ensuring that things are in order or clean. The rituals include things such as cleaning, washing, repeating a phrase or word over and over again, counting certain numbers repetitively, tapping or touching things a certain number of times, and a lot more. Being a part of a ritual makes a kid suffering from OCD find temporary relief from bad thoughts, worry or fear. The more a kid is a part of any ritual, the greater is the urge they feel in doing something over and over again. This makes the kid get stuck in a repetitive cycle.

Teens and kids feel embarrassed as they feel afraid that they may be teased for the rituals that they indulge in. They often hide the rituals that they indulge in and make sure that others do not end up noticing them. It greatly impacts students at school. The urge to rewrite, erase and re-do something can slow down the kids in comparison to others. These kids would not answer a question correctly during a test if it uses a bad word or number as per their imagination. They would rather settle for a poor grade than break their OCD rules. Many parents do not even realize that their child is facing difficulties in leading a normal life.

Scientists are not yet aware of why only a few people get OCD. Kids may develop OCD owing to an infection or because it may be in their genes. Differences in brain activity or structures can as well result in OCD. Such kids have no control over their condition. But the right therapy or diagnosis can help them get better with time.

OCD can get better with the right care and attention. However, things can get worse if an appropriate treatment is not received at the right time. If you think your child has OCD, it is best to talk to your child about what is bothering them. You need to speak to them in a supportive manner and shower them with love. You need to tell them what you have noticed. Reassuring your child that they will be fine and you just want to help them can prove to be soothing.

Kids with OCD often feel embarrassed or ashamed at first. They may deny or try to hide whatever they are doing. However, your child would feel relieved if there is somebody to offer support to them. It is best to schedule a visit to a pediatrician once you have noticed differences in their behavior. You need to encourage your child to speak up. The doctor will ask questions as well as examine your child to determine a diagnosis. This would help the doctor in deciding whether the symptoms could be OCD or any other condition. The doctor may then refer the patient to a mental health professional for further treatment.

It can be a great relief to kids when OCD is diagnosed. This is because they are no longer battling alone. They need some kind of help to let them get better over time. Cognitive behavioral therapy is employed by the therapists for treating OCD. During this therapy, teens and kids learn diverse techniques which can help them. Kids learn how to face fear and resist indulging in rituals. These skills can help in resetting the activity of the brain and adapt a healthier way of living. Medications are also prescribed by a few doctors for treating OCD.

Parents should exercise caution when opting what information they share with their children during treatment, though it is not an easy task. It requires a lot of patience and practice. There can be setbacks and successes along the way. Support and several resources are available for families and parents dealing with OCD. Knowing that you are not alone can help a great deal in coping with this condition.

Risk Factors

More than 25% of Americans are likely to experience anxiety at any stage of their lives. Some of the risks factors involved in OCD are:

Gender

It has been seen that women have somewhat of a higher risk of having mental disorders as compared to men. There can be different factors behind this, such as cultural pressure to meet the needs of everyone except for themselves.

There can also be obstacles where the patient does not disclose all of their symptoms to the doctors. Also, women's emotions vary frequently due to hormone changes during their menstrual cycles, and stress and anxiety during these times may even lead to OCD.

Age

Generally, those with OCD and other mental disorders show early signs during childhood. Talking about the panic disorder and social phobias, they can be diagnosed during one's teenage period. According to some studies, about 3 to 5 percent of kids live with anxiety disorder.

Children and adults having such issues are likely to develop other disorders such as anxiety or depression at a later age.

Personality

The personality of a person plays an important role in determining the risks of this disorder. For example, most of the shy and less confident children are likely to be targeted by bullies in school. Due to this reason, it is suggested that you should try to make your children confident. They should be confident enough to face the world and understand what is right and what is wrong. In this way, they will comprehend the difference between negative and positive thoughts.

They will also have a solid imagination and will not let the negative thoughts overcome them.

Family History

There is no doubt that genetics play an important role in causing OCD. It is known to run in families. Apart from the genetic factor, the psychological influences and dynamics have a major role to play as well. It has been known that kids develop the habits of their parents. If they discover their parents are living with phobias, chances are the children will as well.

Social Factors

Certain social factors can also cause OCD in many people. It has been shown in a study that school and post-secondary students are more likely to suffer from OCD. The numbers have risen significantly since the 1950s. OCD can also be associated with the lack of connections or because of a threatening environment. For example, if your kid doesn't like to go out and feels uncomfortable when he is in a gathering, you need to figure out the right solution for it.

You need to ask yourself, why he is not going out to play? Is there anyone who teases him or bullies him? Has he witnessed some dangerous or unpleasant events?

Traumatic Events

These events are more likely to trigger OCD and other mental disorders, especially in people who are susceptible to them because of the genetic, biochemical or psychological factors. One of the best examples is suffering from OCD because of post-traumatic stress. Certain events in childhood, for example, child abuse or spousal abuse, may lead to the development of mental disorders.

Medical Conditions

There are some medical conditions that may also result in mental disorders like OCD. Some of the common conditions are mitral valve prolapse, chronic fatigue syndrome, obstructive sleep apnea, migraines, premenstrual syndrome and irritable bowel syndrome. There is nothing we can do about the medical history of a person, as it can't be changed.

Certain activities of the brain are also associated with it. It has been seen that there are differences in the structure of the patient's brain and those who are not affected by it. There is some connection, but what it is and where it comes from are still unknown. Medical experts and professionals are trying their best to figure out this connection, but they have not been successful until now. Recognizing the causes will help all of us to determine the personalized and specific treatments of OCD.

There are almost equal chances of OCD's occurrence in males and females, though females are a bit more prone to having this mental disorder. Most of the cases are developed in early childhood or during late adolescence. However, it can occur to anyone at any time of his life.

As soon as some negative thoughts begin to appear in your mind or you feel that it's the first time you are feeling like this, get medical assistance at the earliest opportunity. Living with OCD isn't an easy thing since there are many complications in it. What they need is proper help at the right time.

Living with OCD

Life is very hard for people suffering from OCD and other mental disorders. To many people, living with anxiety is just like a nightmare. In this segment of the article, focus is given on the darkest experiences that Obsessive Compulsive Disorder patients have to face due to the presence of this condition in their lives.

Once Obsessive Compulsive Disorder is confirmed, a patient may experience great mental challenges. The whole span of these challenges can be categorized into three phases generally. The first phase is the initial moments after being diagnosed as an OCD patient. The second phase occurs after the short-lived initial phase. The second stage can extend from a few weeks to a few months. Finally, the third step is recognized as a longer time period and may last a couple of years after being confirmed as an OCD patient. Let's get inside the patient's mind and know what they face during this period.

Initial Stage

This is the stage when most people with Obsessive Compulsive Disorder remain unaware of the disease. They don't even have a clue about the disease at this stage. Though they aren't conscious of their mental problem, often the signs and symptoms of OCD are expressed through their behavior. In the case of one teenager, she confessed that she often had some bizarre thoughts in her mind. It was like after finishing some certain job, she always had something that used to roam in her mind to sort out what she should do next. Though she had quite a big agenda of a to-do list before starting a certain task, she couldn't find out the next one when she finished that job and finally ended up doing nothing.

Another thing that she had to face was a quick shift of her mood in the preliminary stage. Her mood swung very rapidly in this period. She expressed that usually at night she remained in a very depressed mood and felt lonely, detached and silent in the darkness. She couldn't tolerate a single ray of light in that period. On the contrary, in the morning, she became a completely new person. No gloomy and heavy feeling remained in her mind. She seemed to love life. She tried to catch every single bit of rays of the sun around herself. She removed all the window coverings and made her surroundings as lighted as possible. Thus, her mentality twisted and turned in a short period of time.

People like her face the double meaning of everything. It is like they want to find some sort of philosophy in each of their tasks. They always keep asking for answers for their choices. Thus, they create a complex situation inside their mind and end up in doing nothing. This complex level of thinking clouds their minds and judgment.

Another issue they face is that they find the presence of some sort of diabolic entities everywhere. They always feel that some sort of evil lies in everything. Thus, they have constant queries and suspicions in their mind. They can't think or act normal because of these queries. These feelings make them restless, unstable and insomniac. Often they seem to enter into a trance in this process and cause mental disturbance and agony.

Gradually, these behavioral defects become more and more frequent, and at a certain point they reach a certain state where seeking medical help becomes imperative. In this process of seeking medical help, those with OCD come to know about this mental defect in them.

Secondary Stage

The secondary stage of OCD in the patients' lives begins right after the initial stage. The duration of this stage varies from patient to patient. For some, this stage completes only within a couple of weeks. On the other hand, for others, it can be a bit lengthy and they may take a few months to pass this stage. It is the most vulnerable stage of life for an OCD patient. In this stage, we start to suffer the adverse impacts of Obsessive Compulsive Disorder in the full scale. Often those lose the control over their activities and thoughts and involve in harmful activities and cause self-inflicted pain. As they experience this problem with a greater intensity, they always suffer to cope with that. Besides, many also suffer from some sort of mental trauma as they come to know about this.

Though most of us suffer from the symptoms of OCD for a long time, they face a sheer panic when they come to know about their disease formally from a medical expert. Their lives face a drastic change. People around them, including friends and family, may put a deep impact in the patient's life. In a sensitive surrounding where people care about the OCD patients, he or she may find it much more easy to cope with the recurring problems of life.

On the contrary, in a harsh surrounding, many have to suffer a lot just because of the insensitive behavior they have to face. Finally, the secondary stage is very much vital for us as we stay in a touch-and-go situation in this stage.

An ambient environment and positive mentality are required for the betterment of all.

Final Stage

The final stage is the longest stage for a person with OCD. This stage may extend to several years or even decades. By the time we have reached this stage, we've already learned many coping skills. We can be in both a positive or negative state. The matter of sorrow is that the patient's life never becomes the same as it was before.

We lead a systematic life in this stage. Some take medications on a regular basis and attend sessions with psychiatrists. In this phase, many strive to make the illness a part of their lives and try their best to minimize the adverse impacts as much as possible. In this stage, we try to be cautious about the radical thoughts that come across in their minds and try to control these thoughts and in that way control the disease.

Going Through These Stages

The journey that we have to make with this condition is full of twists and turns. A strict mentality and undefeatable fighting spirit and a proper strategy with the combination of medical treatment is required to fight against all the odds presented by OCD.

If we are asked the question regarding how we may fight against the problems created by OCD, most of us would answer that we are not sure yet because we have already made these problems a part of our lives. It is essential that people suffering from OCD don't take it as a burden of their life. This is a disease that stays with a person for their whole life. So there is no benefit in running from it. Rather, we should embrace this illness and take it in the simplest way possible.

Another useful way to deal with the difficulties created by OCD is to be skeptical about realism and surrealism in their day-to-day lives. For most of us, the line that lies between the realistic and surrealistic worlds is often hard to detect. The mind of an OCD patient is often invaded by surrealistic thoughts. These thoughts have no existence in the real life. These thoughts are like voices in our heads, and they scream and provoke the patient's mind towards surrealistic thoughts redundantly. For instance, a vast majority of us have confessed that they imagined random people completely nude in a public place. In order to get free from these disturbing thoughts, we should be more skeptical about the visions they see, imaginary activities they hallucinate and thoughts that come across their minds. In this way, we will gain a resistance against these disturbing thoughts.

Another approach called, forgetting the perfection, has proved to be very useful for the Obsessive Compulsive Disorder patient. As it was discussed before that we are often restrained to some specific physical and mental incapability, we focus to get the necessary things done by the marginal standard rather than focusing on gaining 100% perfection. Though it is a very difficult approach to master in the beginning, as we all want to be perfect, it becomes handy for those suffering from Obsessive Compulsive Disorder in the later stages of their lives.

Another tactic that we find very helpful is the strategic decision making. In this process, the people try their best not to be too judgmental. Those of us try not to be too worried about some particular decision making. They build the simple habit of following the gut feelings. A complicated and thoughtful decision making process is very complex and requires deep thinking. These critical processes put us under severe pressure and may cause concussion and confusion. Rather than playing by the rules during decisions making, we find it easier to do or decide what we think is best for us.

Issues That Haunt Us

Despite the above-mentioned strategies that are often followed widely by those of us with OCD, some people cannot overcome some specific fears throughout their whole lives. Though they try to get rid of the specific horrors more than anything, they can't seem to pull themselves out of these fears. It's like a ghost that haunts them over and over again. A brief discussion of these fears is given below.

Fear of Doing Something Wrong

This is the most horrific feeling that haunts an OCD patient all his or her life. Obsessive Compulsive Disorder sufferers have the tendency of losing control over themselves, they tremble with fear at the thought of doing something wrong at that vulnerable moment.

Unusual Guilty Feeling

We often feel guilty for exhibiting what would be perceived by most as odd behaviour of which they no control. As we always struggle with the insecurity of doing bad things, they also feel guilty for those deeds. It is like a self-inflicted agony as the insecurity is followed by guilty feelings. These feelings also result in depression and thus the depression leads to attacks.

Lack of Sympathy

It is often seen that those suffering from Obsessive Compulsive Disorder receive marginal sympathy from the communities they belong to. It is quite a problematic issue as they need the support from their community. Due to the nature of this mental disorder, people often fail to understand the helplessness. This illness is not like a scar on the face that shows the intensity of a patient's trauma.

Most of the time, we remain in a stable, controlled and sociable state, so most of the community members don't realize the vulnerability of an OCD patient and the actual intensity of this mental disorder.

Identity Crisis

As we often lose control of their minds and feel guilty deep inside, sometimes they suffer from identity crisis. They often create multiple personalities in their minds due to confusion.

Finally, our life is inexplicably tough. Comfort can be gotten if people around an Obsessive Compulsive Disorder person come forward to provide a helping hand. It greatly benefits those who suffer from it when there is support and sensitivity given from friends, family and the community.

Medical Treatment

It is unfortunate that the cure of Obsessive Compulsive Disorder has not been discovered yet in modern medical science. Though there is no complete remedy for Obsessive Compulsive Disorder, it can be controlled by making certain lifestyle changes. There are basically two conventional ways of treating a person with this illness. The first method is psychotherapy and the second one is medications. Sometimes, doctors require a combination of both methods to treat a patient. In most cases, the treatment of is a lifelong process. Both of these methods used to treat OCD are described below:

Psychotherapy

Psychotherapy, also known as Cognitive Behavioral Therapy (CBT), is the first step in treating OCD. CBT is an Exposure and Response Prevention process. In this therapy process, we must face the very objects or persons, abstract ideas or situations they fear most. In this process, people interact with their fears repeatedly, thus coming across the feared things continuously can swipe away all the fear.

Cognitive Behavioral Therapy is administrated in a systematic process. The first step of this process is to identify the patient's behavioral defects. Kanfer and Saslow developed a four-step model to assess the cognitive behavioral defects, which are:

> Identifying critical behaviors.
> Determining the degree of critical behavior.
> Evaluating critical behavior.
> Trying to fix the problem.

In the first step, a therapist must identify the catalysts that trigger OCD in a patient's mind. Here, the therapist tries to recognize the stimulus that creates an adverse effect in the patient's mind. In the second step, the therapist observes the patient's reactions to the stimulus and tries to determine whether the reactions are too minimal or too much. In the third step, the therapist tries to evaluate how deeply these reactions affect an OCD patient. The therapist tries to detect how often we are victimized by the disorder and how adversely it attacks. Finally, in the fourth and last step, the therapist exposes the patient to a certain stimulus that triggers a sense of fear, nervousness and unease in his mind.

Though the model developed by Kanfer and Saslow is a widely used method for CBT, different forms of CBT are used by the psychiatrists. Another method of CBT was proposed by Hofmann which is also very popular for treating this illness. This process consists of six phases:

Psychological assessment.
Reconceptualization.
Skill acquisition.
Skill consolidation and application training.
Generalization and assessment.
Post-treatment assessment and follow-up.

The whole process of CBT therapy requires consistency and a lot of patience to bring a fruitful result. These therapy sessions can be administered personally or in group. Finally, CBT is a very useful and scientific medical tool for psychiatrists as treatment.

Medication

The most common medication prescribed are Selective Serotonin Reuptake Inhibitors (SSRIs). SSRIs are drugs used to get rid of depression. Besides SSRIs, Clomipramine of the tricyclic antidepressants class is also used as the prescribed medicine for OCD. There are some other drugs available in the market for the treatment of OCD. Below is a short list of FDA-approved drugs that can be administered:

> Sertraline (Zoloft)
> Fluvoxamine
> Paroxetine (Paxil)
> Citalopram (Celexa)
> Fluoxetine (Prozac)
> Escitalopram (Lexapro)

Among the above-mentioned medication, most of them can be administered to both children and adults, with the exception of Paroxetine (Paxil). Paroxetine (Paxil) should only be administrated to adults.

The above-stated medications used are mostly slow-burner type. Usually, these medications take around two to two-and-a-half months to have effect on the patient. In some cases, it takes a shorter time to get the benefits of these medications. In this regard, the best case scenario is that we get relief from OCD within a month of taking medications. An important thing would be that in all circumstances, these medications must be taken under the close and direct supervision of a well-trained and certified doctor.

It is widely known that many drugs used for remedies have certain minor side effects; drugs used for OCD are no exception. These drugs should be administered and taken cautiously while keeping some certain issues in mind. There are some issues given below that should be taken into consideration while advising and consuming these drugs.

Like every medicine, these drugs have some particular side effects. Nausea, restlessness, dizziness, insomnia, erectile dysfunction, and weight gain are some of the common side effects. A doctor must make sufferers aware of these side effects and offer them some advice to minimize the adverse impacts of these side effects.

Another important issue to consider is sorting out the best medications for a particular OCD patient. As stated above, drugs come with some side effects; the severity of these side effects may vary from patient to patient. Moreover, all people may not find the same drug equally useful. So it is an important duty of any doctor to find out the best suited medicine for every patient.

The third issue is very important for both the patients and the doctors. Sometimes the drugs used may trigger some inappropriate thoughts among us. Generally, younger children suffer from this problem. Though most of the drugs used for the treatment of OCD are beyond this risk, the FDA has strictly ordered the drug manufacturers to add proper caution statements with these drugs.

Finally, medication is a very effective solution for treatment. Research has shown that around 20% of those with OCD get relief from this disorder after taking these medications.

Behavioral Therapy

With the advancement of medical science, very little progression has been made in the field of treatment for those suffering from Obsessive Compulsive Disorder. Doctors still rely on the traditional methods. Among the widely used methods is behavioral therapy.

This form of treatment is very effective for those who are suffering in the primary stage. In this article, an explanation will be made to elaborate on all the pros and cons of behavioral therapy.

Cognitive Behavioral Therapy

The most useful therapy that provides a positive impact is Cognitive Behavioral Therapy commonly known as CBT. There is a big difference between the traditional psychological therapy and CBT. In most cases of traditional psychological therapy, the doctor and the patient converse with each other. In traditional therapy sessions, the patient expresses his or her problematic mental states and disturbing mental experiences. The doctor then provide aids, based on their mental disorder.

On the other hand, CBT is very effective from both the patient's and doctor's points of view. In a CBT session, both the doctor and the patient have certain roles to play. CBT utilizes two different and significant approaches. The first one is using the cognitive therapy. It depicts the way we see and relate to everything around us. The second one is the behavioral therapy that attempts to answer the question as to how the experiences influence our ways of thinking and performing.

A basic strategy often used to perform CBT is the process of "Exposure and Response Prevention". It is also known as the ERP method. In this strategy, psychiatrists take necessary initiatives to remove some default feelings in the patient's mind. It is known that this disorder creates some feelings of fear, anxiety, unease and phobias of some absurd objects, situations, persons and places in the patient's mind. In the ERP method, a therapist tries to recreate the environment in which OCD triggers the certain feelings of fear, anxiety or unease and makes the patient experience the situation.

Therapists experiment with a patient's psyche by recreating these situations again and again. Continuous exposure of the same type of situation builds a resistance in the mind of the patient. He or she can remove all the fears, anxieties and phobias that used to haunt him or her previously and get rid of OCD for the long term.

A sub-segment of ERP is also used as a tool to treat. This sub- segment is referred as *imaginal exposure*. In this process, various scripts are written based on a patient's default mental experiences. These written scripts are used repeatedly with the patient so that they can learn about their fear and anxieties. By knowing and experiencing their fears, they can conquer them.

A person suffering from OCD doesn't see everything the way we do. Usually, we possess a heterogeneous vision, thoughts about things which have no parity with reality. In CBT therapy sessions, doctors try to get into the imaginary world of their patients and bring them back into the real world. It is like turning the patient's mind upside down. It can be stressful and problematic for the patient. Therefore, a doctor must proceed with caution when utilizing this method. The focus of the primary sessions of CBT should be on discovering which motives cause the symptoms of an OCD patient, thus helping the patient to better understand how CBT works.

There are a few strategies a doctor may have at his or her disposal that he or she may use to provide therapy to an OCD patient. Four basic strategies should be mentioned which can be used for CBT. A brief description of them is given below:

The rewind technique: This is a widely used technique. In this method, we are asked to bring back the memories of their fear and anxiety while they are in a safe, controlled environment and under the doctor's supervision. During this technique, we feel the tension and stress at first, and then the therapist helps them to be relaxed again. Doctors use this therapy repeatedly until minimal stress in our minds about any particular fear or phobia.

Differentiating the patient's psychology from OCD: In this technique, a doctor tries to separate the patient from the disorder. The patient is required to understand that OCD is a small part of their behavioral habits and not the whole picture. One should proceed with caution as the quicker a patient's identity is separated from it, the more likely the patient will overcome it.

Breaking the pattern: If we take a closer look at the cases of sufferers, we will see that they have an identical manner of doing similar things repeatedly. Thus, people suffering from OCD develop a behavioral pattern. A doctor or a therapist is required to break down behavioral patterns. A doctor should be able to make you understand that your behaviors are not fixed and static, and these behaviors should be changed if they are harming your lives. Doctors or therapists can assign various tasks to help break behavioral patterns.

Hypnosis: Aside from being fearful, it is also reported that OCD causes hypnosis. It is often seen that people suffering from this illness indulges in a certain activity and forget about the rest of the world. OCD sometimes brings patients into a trance. In these cases, therapists can use hypnosis and make them imagine doing some certain activities they fear to do. In this way, therapists can break the negative impacts.

Finally, Cognitive Behavioral Therapy is a very effective treatment method for people with Obsessive Compulsive Disorder. Research has shown that a staggering 75% of OCD patients are benefiting from Cognitive Behavioral Therapy.

Self-Treatment & Care

Understanding and Treating Anxiety

One of the main reasons for OCD is anxiety. Understanding anxiety will certainly help in the treatment.

Normal anxiety is understandable and we can say that it is a part of our evolution. It is better to be anxious than to be overconfident. Normal people have a moderate amount of anxiety that keeps them safe and helps avert danger.

When this threshold of normal anxiety is disturbed, problems arise and this anxiety turns into panic attacks and phobias. Panic attacks cause extreme anxiety and even feelings of terror. During panic attacks, people usually experience shortness of breath, choking feeling, chest pain or racing of the heart. Phobias are fears about specific things or objects.

Anxiety can be treated by managing stress. Some of the stress management techniques include:

Progressive Muscle Relaxation Technique – Here, particular muscles like your neck and shoulder muscles are first tensed and then relaxed.

Calming Counts is when a patient closes his eyes as they inhale and exhale.

Breathing exercise.

Meditation.

Healthy diet – a poor diet increases moodiness and fatigue that turn into anxiety and stress. Foods that beat anxiety are foods that are high in vitamin B (e.g. poultry and green leafy vegetables), high in antioxidants (like fresh vegetables and fruits), dairy products, foods with omega-3 fats (fish, like salmon), coconut and olive oil, and magnesium-rich foods (such as leafy vegetables, beans, yogurt, bananas, nuts, etc.).

Get enough sleep.

Obsession means images or thoughts that continuously preoccupy the mind even when we try to keep these away. To overcome these obsessions, compulsion rituals are performed because our obsessions force us to behave or act in that way. Vicious cycle of OCD:

Obsessive thought is triggered.

It takes the form of anxiety.

Compulsive urges to give meaning to that obsession.

Temporary relief.

Obsessive thought is triggered.

By treating these obsessions and compulsions we can treat the cruel cycle of OCD:

It is said that where your mind goes, the energy flows.

Start thinking differently and start challenging your thoughts. It's not necessary to believe in everything that you think.

Challenge yourself to counter your thoughts and to think in some other way or some new thought. If your thought is negative, try to make it positive. Always try to think of a situation that will have a positive outcome.

You can always make some new and pleasant thoughts that will make you happy and distract your mind.

Even if you fail in doing so, don't worry, just try again. Don't try to judge yourself. Simply repeat it every time you fail.

Take full responsibility. When you feel responsible for your situation, you will automatically feel more able to solve your problem.

Another way to cope is trying not to think. This can be achieved by being mindfulness. Just try be in the present. Whatever you are doing, focus fully on that. Keep asking yourself, "What am I doing now?" This will keep you focused.

Resist the Urges

Face your fears and don't try to avoid these. Start analyzing things that cause anxiety and fear which may lead to obsessions and compulsions. Focus your attention on it and analyze how many times and with what intensity the fear or urge arises:

Delay that urge of compulsion. It will be difficult in the beginning, but being dedicated to practice it will become easier. For example, if there is an urge to wash your hands repeatedly, delay it. Control the urge and try to resist it altogether.

Try to refocus that attention into other things, like exercising, dancing, singing, playing, reading or any other activities you like.

Practice these steps with dedication and bravery. Be true to yourself and never try to feel inferior about yourself. The truer you are to yourself, the more you will improve.

Accept Help

There is a therapy called family therapy that is useful in fighting OCD. Talking to family members promotes understanding among all the family members.

Don't be afraid to ask for help. Talk to someone that will definitely help you. Even talking to someone can minimize the urge.

Avoid being alone. Being amongst people will help you avoid those thoughts and be at ease. Spend more time with family and friends.

Talk to people who are suffering from OCD and share your experiences with them. In this way, people with similar experiences will be able to support each other. This will have many benefits like feelings of acceptance, increased self-confidence, not feeling isolated, you will not feel judged by people, and you will be able to get new information that will help you overcome your problem.

People with mild OCD can use self-help resources for developing their own coping strategies.

Avoid Caffeine and Alcohol

Caffeine and alcohol are temporary stress busters that make things even more complicated. Even if you feel good and relaxed after consuming them, avoid them because you may get addicted to them. And when these temporary solutions are not available, you may experience headaches and may find it hard to concentrate.

Avoid Sugar Products

Sugar has the capability to change the entire chemical structure of the brain. It can upset naturally occurring calming neuro-transmitter hormones that are needed for healthy brain functioning. These include dopamine, serotonin and GABA.

Sugar leads to a huge high (from a rush of dopamine), but when the sugar leaves the bloodstream, it leaves your body with much less dopamine and serotonin. Both of these hormones work together to promote a healthy mood, and while some drugs treat low serotonin, they can't do much good when you're constantly feeding your body more poison. The medication may not work effectively if sugar is consumed.

Initial Treatment

The most effective counseling type for OCD is Exposure and Response Prevention (ERP). In this, the person suffering from OCD is deliberately exposed to an obsession he is dealing with. This should be done under the expert guidance of a therapist or a doctor.

In this type of counseling, the patient is supposed to write all the obsessions and the behaviours that follow these. Analyze and arrange the obsession on the basis of the fear that accompanies that obsession. For example, the obsession that creates maximum anxiety and fear is on the top of the list and the one with minimum anxiety is at the bottom. With the help of a therapist, the patient starts confronting and working on the obsessions that create minimum stress to the obsessions that create maximum stress.

This therapy is also known as cognitive behavioral therapy, which is a type of psychotherapy. There are more intensive counseling programs, like group counseling, full day counseling or sometimes hospitalizing the patient for some time.

Treatment by Medications

As mentioned earlier, medication therapy includes prescribing an antidepressant called a selective serotonin reuptake inhibitor (SSRI), such as Fluoxetine (for example, Prozac) or a tricyclic antidepressant, such as Clomipramine. Results may be seen within 1 to 3 weeks. But for proper improvement and good results, it can take as many as 12 weeks.

Some of the approved antidepressants to treat OCD are Clomipramine (Anafranil), Fluoxetine (Prozac), Paroxetine (Paxil, Pexeva) and Sertraline (Zoloft). On the other hand, some of the possible side effects of selective serotonin reuptake inhibitors (SSRI) are feeling agitated, feeling sick, constipation, dizziness, headache or insomnia.

Nutritional Therapy

The nutritional or herbal therapy focuses on boosting natural serotonin levels and GABA levels. These are two neurotransmitters that help in minimizing the worrying or anxiety thoughts.

L-theanine is an amino acid found in tea. It has a calming and anti-anxiety affect. It increases alpha waves that are associated with creating a calm state within 40 minutes of ingestion.

Other nutritional resources include:

Free Form Amino-Acid Complex
Omega-3 Fatty Acid
B-100 Complex
Gamma-aminobutyric Acid (GABA)
N,N-Dimethylglycine
Inositol
5-hydroxytryptophan (5-HTP)
St. John's Wort (Hypericum Perforatum)
Valerian Root Extract
Passion Flower
Kava
Chamomile Tea
Hops
Lemon Balm
DHEA

The Inositol Treatment

Inositol, a type of vitamin B, is effective in treating OCD. Inositol is used in biochemical processes that effect serotonin receptors.

Severe OCD Treatments

Brain Surgery: There are two types of brain surgeries. The first is Anterior cingulotomy and the second one is Anterior capsulotomy.

Gamma Knife: Multiple gamma rays are passed through the skull to destroy the targeted brain tissue. This procedure is called ventral capsulotomy.

Deep Brain Stimulation (DBS): DBS involves placing electrodes in targeted areas of the brain and connecting them by wires under the skin to pulse generators. These pulse generators, also known as "implantable neuro-stimulators," contain a battery for power and a microchip to control the stimulation.

Research on New Medication Options: Here, Glutamate is targeted which is the most abundant neurotransmitter.

Useful Contacts

Those suffering from OCD can find help in different ways. There are many organizations spread all over the world that are working for the better health of us. There are also many support groups and survivor societies running in different places around the world. Another sector has recently come forward to play the role of a pioneer in providing support to people with this disorder. This particular sector is the internet. There are numerous websites and blogs about OCD available on the internet.

These websites and blogs publish contents of journals and research papers written and published by medical experts. It is of great help to them and their families. With the help of these websites and blogs, people can learn the expert's opinion regarding OCD and its treatment methods from home. Now, let's get introduced to some of the contacts via which we can get help.

Organizations

Several organizations are providing aid to the people who are suffering from OCD and their families. Some of them are mentioned below for your convenience.

International OCD Foundation
PO Box: 961029
E-mail: info@iocdf.org
Phone: 617-973-5801

Anxiety Disorders Association of America
Phone: 240-485-1001
Fax: 240-485-1035
E-mail: information@adaa.org

Mental Health America
Phone: 800-969-6642
Fax: 703-684-5968

National Institute on Mental Health
Phone: 866-615-6464
E-mail: nimhinfo@nih.gov
Fax: 301-443-4279

American Psychiatry Organization
Phone: 703-907-7300
E-mail: apa@psych.org

An amazing fact about these organizations is that most of them work voluntarily and are funded by the government, so there should be no hesitation in asking for help from these organizations. All that is required of an OCD patient is to contact one of these organizations in order to seek help.

Conclusion

OCD is a mental disorder involving thoughts which are persistent, intrusive and seem inappropriate, causing high levels of distress and worry. There is a high risk of OCD being present in the offspring of someone suffering from this illness.

If it is discovered that someone in the family has OCD, there is a high probability that other members may also have it. Hence, it shows there is hereditary involvement in this illness. Thoughts relating to insecurities may be common, like doors not being locked or getting contaminated by shaking hands, and things or items in disorder. They feel it is mandatory to fix these things by keeping all their belongings in order, checking things often, regularly washing hands, etc. Studies regarding analyzing genes for this disease are being conducted to identify this disorder's nature and to help us overcome it with effective treatments.

Thank you very much for buying this book. It really is appreciated. Please take a moment to write a brief review if you purchased it online.

Katie

References

Canadian Mental Health
https://cmha.ca/documents/obsessive-compulsive-disorder-ocd/
AnxietyBC
https://www.anxietybc.com/parenting/obsessive-compulsive-disorder
Centre for Addiction and Mental Health
http://www.camh.ca/en/hospital/health_information/a_z_mental_health_and_addiction_information/obsessive_compulsive_disorder/obsessive_compulsive_disorder_information_guide/Pages/ocd_whatis.aspx
Web MD
https://www.webmd.com/mental-health/obsessive-compulsive-disorder#1
Mic Network
https://mic.com/articles/138668/ocd-facts-and-myths-here-s-what-you-should-know-about-obsessive-compulsive-disorder#.bi2mFXrYo
Stopping the Noise in Your Head by Reid Wilson
ISBN-13: 978-0757319068
Obsessive Compulsive Foundation of Metropolitan Chicago
https://adaa.org/sites/default/files/How-to-Help-Your-Child-A-Parents-Guide-to-OCD.pdf